To Kate & Darcy,
Keep on dreaming until your dreams come true! :)

Be Good. Do Good. Dream BIG!
LOVE, JAKE

This book belongs to:

Name_____Age_____

One of my wildest dreams was:

_____

_____

All rights reserved. No part of this book may be reproduced, distributed, stored in a retrieval system, or transmitted in any form, by any means, including mechanical, electronic, photocopying, recording, or otherwise, without the prior written consent of the publisher except in the case of brief quotations embodied in critical reviews or certain other noncommercial uses permitted by copyright law.

Published by Jake's World
Words ©2021 Chris Hardy
Illustrations ©2021 Wally_LL (Osipova V.)

Library of Congress Number: 2021909889
ISBN: 978-1-7363235-4-0
Printed in the United States
First printing 2021

Jake's World
1407 Foothill Blvd., #134
La Verne, CA 91750
www.jakesbigworld.com
Email: jake@jakesbigworld.com
Insta/Facebook: @jakesbigworld2020

Chris Hardy's first book, *Jake and the Pandemic,* was a wonderful success as a heartwarming keepsake that put smiles on the faces of many children and adults alike. *The Purple Unicorn* is her follow-up book which is pure fun, adventure & craziness. Her upcoming books include a lizard pursuing his life-long dream, a kitty cat dealing with fear and a squirrel who's more interested in playing around than being responsible. Plenty of adventures are just around the corner in Jake's World!

Victoria "Wally_LL" Osipova is a Russian designer & illustrator who has been creating children's illustrations since 2015. Wally_LL also illustrated *Jake and the Pandemic* and is currently working on Jake's upcoming book, *Grateful Jake*.

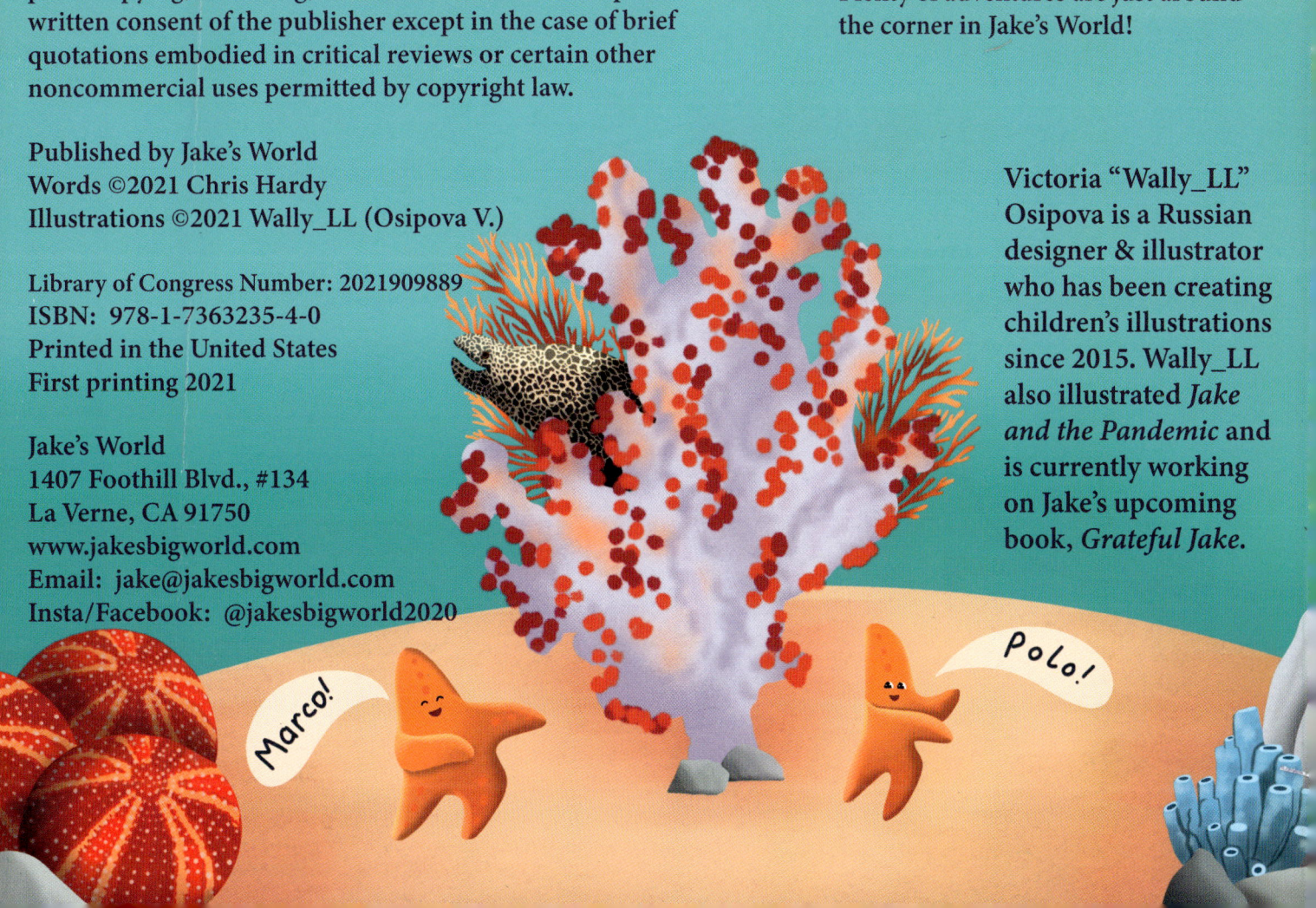

Jake's Dreamland
Jake and the Purple Unicorn

by
Chris Hardy

illustrated by
Wally_LL (Osipova V.)

Dedicated to everyone who has ridiculously silly dreams...

To my crazy friends and family... you know who you are!
Don't ever change!

What a fun day that little Jake had, running around the block...

...so once his head hit the bed, it now was dream o'clock.

"Oh boy," said Jake, who's still not awake, "what can I do today?"

He thought he'd go and try to find someone with whom to play.

The streets were empty, not a creature in sight for miles on down the road.

So Jake took a left and then a right and found his friend Tedd the toad.

Lucky for Jake, this happened to be the smartest toad near and far.

Tedd knew of a place where Jake could go so he said he'd lend him his car.

They got to a forest so green and big and then they said goodbye.

Tedd patted Jake's back and wished him luck as he gave him a wink of his eye.

Jake walked through the forest and yelled out "hello" hoping to find a friend.

Out from the shadows a big purple creature said, "Hi, my name is Gwen."

She said they could go on a wild adventure and of course Jake said, "Let's go!"

He jumped on her back, held on for dear life as he saw the ground below.

She swished and swashed and wished and washed while Jake yelled out "Oh no!"

The next thing he knows they started to go straight towards the ocean below!

They went under the sea, that unicorn and he, wondering what they would find.

There were so many things they couldn't believe or get them out of their minds.

They saw wizards and lizards...

...and goats on floats.

They saw sharks named Mark...

...and seals with wheels.

They saw whales who were knitting and otters just sitting.

They saw basketball teams and Stuart with ice cream.

There was so much to see, Jake's head filled with glee, and he didn't want to leave!

But Gwen then said, her horn to his head, "Well, this isn't up to me."

"I've taken you on a ride for the night but morning is on its way."

"It's time to get you back into bed so you can start your day."

Jake awakened soon after and looked at his mom who had a quizzical look. "My goodness, dear baby, where did your dreams take you...and what is this nautical hook???"

Jake thought where he bought that necklace he wore, but none of it seemed to make sense. "Am I really awake or am I still dreaming?" he wondered while kept in suspense.

Jake put his head down on his pillow of blue, thinking and wishing he knew. But he had no clue what was really true... so tell me, dear friend.....do you??